PIANO SOLO

BLESSED ASSURANCE

The Gospel Hymns of FANNY J. CROSBY

Arranged by Cindy Berry

ISBN 978-1-4803-4000-8

Shawnee Press

EXCLUSIVELY DISTRIBUTED BY

HAL•LEONARD®
CORPORATION
7777 W. BLUEMOUND RD. P.O. BOX 13819 MILWAUKEE, WI 53213

In Australia Contact:
Hal Leonard Australia Pty. Ltd.
4 Lentara Court
Cheltenham, Victoria, 3192 Australia
Email: ausadmin@halleonard.com.au

Visit Hal Leonard Online at
www.halleonard.com

Visit Shawnee Press Online at
www.shawneepress.com

ALL THE WAY MY SAVIOR LEADS ME

Arranged by
CINDY BERRY

Words by FANNY J. CROSBY
Music by ROBERT LOWRY

4

I AM THINE, O LORD

Arranged by
CINDY BERRY

Words by FANNY J. CROSBY
Music by WILLIAM H. DOANE

6

BLESSED ASSURANCE

Arranged by
CINDY BERRY

Lyrics by FANNY J. CROSBY
Music by PHOEBE PALMER KNAPP

Gently, with rubato (♩. = ca. 63)

JESUS IS TENDERLY CALLING

Arranged by
CINDY BERRY

Words by FANNY J. CROSBY
Music by GEORGE C. STEBBINS

PRAISE HIM! PRAISE HIM!

Arranged by
CINDY BERRY

Words by FANNY J. CROSBY
Music by CHESTER G. ALLEN

With a Celtic feel (♩. = ca. 72)

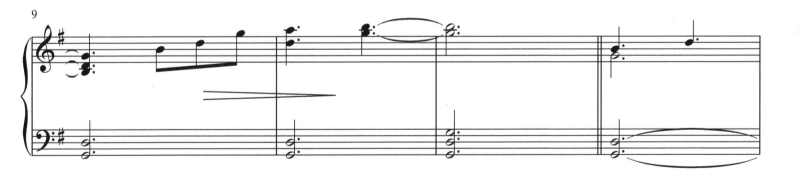

NEAR THE CROSS

Arranged by
CINDY BERRY

Words by FANNY J. CROSBY
Music by WILLIAM H. DOANE

REDEEMED

Arranged by
CINDY BERRY

Words by FANNY J. CROSBY
Music by WILLIAM J. KIRKPATRICK

RESCUE THE PERISHING

Arranged by
CINDY BERRY

Words by FANNY J. CROSBY
Music by WILLIAM H. DOANE

TO GOD BE THE GLORY

Arranged by
CINDY BERRY

Words by FANNY J. CROSBY
Music by WILLIAM H. DOANE

TELL ME THE STORY OF JESUS

Arranged by
CINDY BERRY

Words by FANNY J. CROSBY
Music by JOHN R. SWENEY

The Best
Sacred Collections
for Piano

Blended Worship Piano Collection

Songs include: Amazing Grace (My Chains Are Gone)
• Be Thou My Vision • I Will Rise • Joyful, Joyful, We
Adore Thee • Lamb of God • Majesty • Open the Eyes
of My Heart • Praise to the Lord, the Almighty • Shout
to the Lord • 10,000 Reasons (Bless the Lord) • Worthy
Is the Lamb • Your Name • and more.
00293528 Piano Solo $17.99

Hymn Anthology

A beautiful collection of 60 hymns arranged for piano
solo, including: Abide with Me • Be Thou My Vision
• Come, Thou Fount of Every Blessing • Doxology •
For the Beauty of the Earth • God of Grace and God
of Glory • Holy, Holy, Holy • It Is Well with My Soul
• Joyful, Joyful, We Adore Thee • Let Us Break Bread
Together • A Mighty Fortress Is Our God • O God, Our
Help in Ages Past • Savior, like a Shepherd Lead Us •
To God Be the Glory • What a Friend We Have in Jesus
• and more.
00251244 Piano Solo $16.99

The Hymn Collection

arranged by Phillip Keveren

17 beloved hymns expertly and beautifully arranged for
solo piano by Phillip Keveren. Includes: All Hail the
Power of Jesus' Name • I Love to Tell the Story • I Surrender All • I've Got Peace Like a River • Were You
There? • and more.
00311071 Piano Solo $14.99

Hymn Duets

arranged by Phillip Keveren

Includes lovely duet arrangements of: All Creatures of
Our God and King • I Surrender All • It Is Well with
My Soul • O Sacred Head, Now Wounded • Praise to
the Lord, The Almighty • Rejoice, The Lord Is King •
and more.
00311544 Piano Duet............................$14.99

Hymn Medleys

arranged by Phillip Keveren

Great medleys resonate with the human spirit, as do the
truths in these moving hymns. Here Phillip Keveren
combines 24 timeless favorites into eight lovely medleys for solo piano.
00311349 Piano Solo $14.99

Hymns for Two

arranged by Carol Klose

12 piano duet arrangements of favorite hymns: Amazing
Grace • Be Thou My Vision • Crown Him with Many
Crowns • Fairest Lord Jesus • Holy, Holy, Holy • I Need
Thee Every Hour • O Worship the King • What a Friend
We Have in Jesus • and more.
00290544 Piano Duet............................$12.99

It Is Well
10 BELOVED HYMNS FOR MEMORIAL SERVICES
arr. John Purifoy

10 peaceful, soul-stirring hymn settings appropriate for
memorial services and general worship use. Titles include: Abide with Me • Amazing Grace • Be Still My
Soul • For All the Saints • His Eye Is on the Sparrow • In
the Garden • It Is Well with My Soul • Like a River Glo-
rious • Rock of Ages • What a Friend We Have in Jesus.
00118920 Piano Solo $12.99

Ragtime Gospel Classics

arr. Steven K. Tedesco

A dozen old-time gospel favorites: Because He Lives
• Goodbye World Goodbye • He Touched Me • I Saw
the Light • I'll Fly Away • Keep on the Firing Line •
Mansion over the Hilltop • No One Ever Cared for Me
like Jesus • There Will Be Peace in the Valley for Me
• Victory in Jesus • What a Day That Will Be • Where
Could I Go.
00142449 Piano Solo $11.99

Ragtime Gospel Hymns

arranged by Steven Tedesco

15 traditional gospel hymns, including: At Calvary
• Footsteps of Jesus • Just a Closer Walk with Thee •
Leaning on the Everlasting Arms • What a Friend We
Have in Jesus • When We All Get to Heaven • and more.
00311763 Piano Solo $10.99

Sacred Classics for Solo Piano

arr. John Purifoy

10 timeless songs of faith, masterfully arranged by John
Purifoy. Because He Lives • Easter Song • Glorify Thy
Name • Here Am I, Send Me • I'd Rather Have Jesus
• Majesty • On Eagle's Wings • There's Something
About That Name • We Shall Behold Him • Worthy Is
the Lamb.
00141703 Piano Solo $14.99

Raise Your Hands
PIANO SOLOS FOR BLENDED WORSHIP
arr. Heather Sorenson

10 uplifting and worshipful solos crafted by Heather Sorenson. Come Thou Fount, Come Thou King • God of Heaven
• Holy Is the Lord (with "Holy, Holy, Holy") • Holy Spirit •
I Will Rise • In Christ Alone • Raise Your Hands • Revela-
tion Song • 10,000 Reasons (Bless the Lord) • Your Name
(with "All Hail the Power of Jesus' Name").
00231579 Piano Solo $14.99

Seasonal Sunday Solos for Piano

24 blended selections grouped by occasion. Includes:
Breath of Heaven (Mary's Song) • Come, Ye Thank-
ful People, Come • Do You Hear What I Hear • God of
Our Fathers • In the Name of the Lord • Mary, Did You
Know? • Mighty to Save • Spirit of the Living God • The
Wonderful Cross • and more.
00311971 Piano Solo $16.99

Sunday Solos for Piano

30 blended selections, perfect for the church pianist. Songs
include: All Hail the Power of Jesus' Name • Be Thou My
Vision • Great Is the Lord • Here I Am to Worship • Majesty • Open the Eyes of My Heart • and many more.
00311272 Piano Solo $17.99

More Sunday Solos for Piano

A follow-up to *Sunday Solos for Piano*, this collection features 30 more blended selections perfect for
the church pianist. Includes: Agnus Dei • Come, Thou
Fount of Every Blessing • The Heart of Worship • How
Great Thou Art • Immortal, Invisible • O Worship the
King • Shout to the Lord • Thy Word • We Fall Down
• and more.
00311864 Piano Solo $16.99

Even More Sunday Solos for Piano

30 blended selections, including: Ancient Words •
Brethren, We Have Met to Worship • How Great Is Our
God • Lead On, O King Eternal • Offering • Savior, Like
a Shepherd Lead Us • We Bow Down • Worthy of Worship • and more.
00312098 Piano Solo $16.99

www.halleonard.com

P/V/G = Piano/Vocal/Guitar arrangements.

Prices, contents and availability subject to change without notice.

0122
001